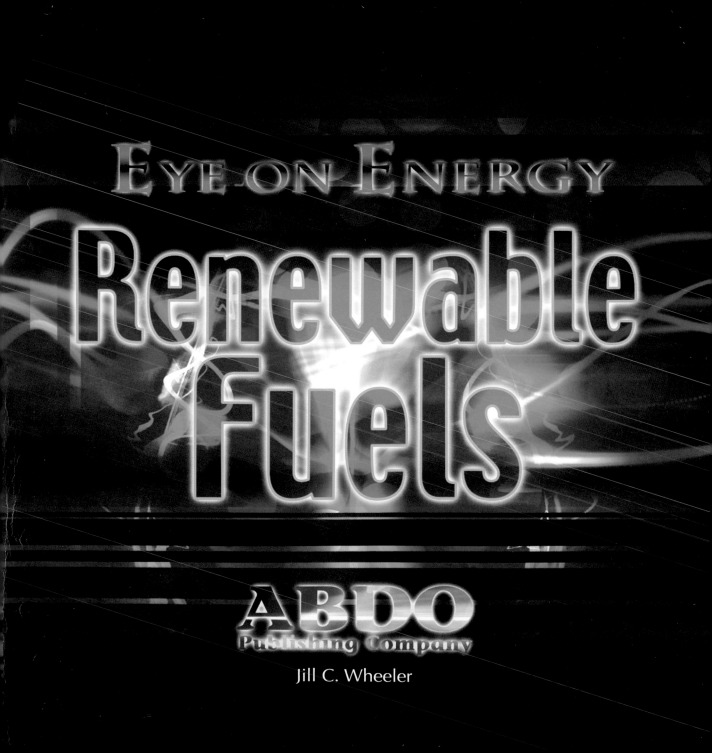

EYE·ON ENERGY

Renewable Fuels

ABDO
Publishing Company

Jill C. Wheeler

visit us at
www.abdopublishing.com

Published by ABDO Publishing Company, 8000 West 78th Street, Edina, Minnesota 55439.
Copyright © 2008 by Abdo Consulting Group, Inc. International copyrights reserved in all
countries. No part of this book may be reproduced in any form without written permission from the
publisher. The Checkerboard Library™ is a trademark and logo of ABDO Publishing Company.

Printed in the United States.

Cover Photo: AP Images
Interior Photos: Alamy pp. 5, 12, 14, 18, 26; AP Images pp. 6, 19, 21, 24, 25, 27, 29; Corbis pp. 4,
    9, 10-11, 17, 20; David R. Frazier/Photo Researchers, Inc. p. 23; Getty Images pp. 7, 15, 16, 22;
    iStockphoto p. 29; Library of Congress pp. 8, 28

Series Coordinator: Rochelle Baltzer
Editors: Rochelle Baltzer, Megan M. Gunderson
Art Direction & Cover Design: Neil Klinepier

Library of Congress Cataloging-in-Publication Data

Wheeler, Jill C., 1964-
  Renewable fuels / Jill C. Wheeler.
    p. cm. – (Eye on energy)
  Includes index.
  ISBN 978–1–59928–808–6
  1. Renewable energy sources–Juvenile literature. I. Title.

  TJ808.2.W45 2007
  621.042–dc22

                                                      2007007110

CONTENTS

FUEL FRENZY

The United States runs on large amounts of fuel. For example, Americans make up about 5 percent of the global population. Yet, they use 25 percent of the world's **petroleum**.

Most of that petroleum is burned as gasoline and diesel fuel in cars and trucks. Each year, Americans burn about 140 billion gallons (530 billion L) of gasoline and 40 billion gallons (150 billion L) of diesel fuel. That's enough fuel to drive an average U.S. car around the world nearly 2 billion times!

Sport-utility vehicles (SUVs) are popular in the United States. However, typical SUVs have about a 40 percent higher carbon dioxide emissions rate than average cars.

Rising gasoline prices and concerns about **global warming** have increased national interest in renewable fuels. Renewable fuels can be replaced more easily than **fossil fuels**.

Plant-based renewable fuels such as ethanol and biodiesel have another major advantage over **fossil fuels**. They are considered "carbon neutral." That means the fuels **emit** the same amount of **carbon dioxide** when burned as the amount absorbed by the plants used to make them.

As plants grow, they absorb carbon dioxide from the air in a process called photosynthesis. Therefore, the making of plant-based fuels reduces carbon dioxide.

FACT OR FICTION?

Renewable fuels, such as ethanol and biodiesel, cannot be used in standard automobile engines.

Fiction. It depends on the fuel blend. Regular vehicles cannot use pure ethanol or biodiesel. But, they can use blends of 10 percent ethanol and 90 percent gasoline. Flexible-fuel cars can use E85, or 85 percent ethanol and 15 percent gasoline. And, most diesel engines can use blends of regular diesel fuel and up to 20 percent biodiesel.

In comparison, **fossil fuels** only add **carbon dioxide** to the **environment**.

Just because a fuel is renewable does not mean it is perfect. Renewable fuels must also be convenient and affordable. Otherwise, most people will not use them.

British Petroleum (BP) became the world's largest oil company when it merged with the Amoco Corporation of the United States in 1998.

Petroleum companies have been operating for more than 100 years. During this time, they have studied the best ways to find, **refine**, and transport petroleum. Renewable fuels companies are just beginning to learn the best ways to operate. They will likely become more **efficient** over time.

During the oil embargo, some gasoline stations had no fuel. At other stations, drivers waited in long lines to fill up.

THE 1973 OIL CRISIS

Summer 2006 was not the first time American consumers faced high gasoline prices. A similar event took place in the early 1970s. In 1973, the Yom Kippur War sparked an oil shortage. The war itself only lasted about three weeks in October 1973. However, its impact lasted for years.

Egypt and Syria fought Israel in the Yom Kippur War. The United States supported Israel, which upset many Arab nations. In protest, a group of oil-exporting Arab nations decided to impose an embargo. They stopped selling oil to the United States and some other countries that had supported Israel during the war.

This decision had a global economic impact. In the United States, the price of oil jumped from about $3 to $12 per barrel.

Americans responded by driving less. They also took more interest in fuel-efficient cars. To reduce gas consumption, Congress lowered the national speed limit from 70 miles per hour (113 km/h) to 55 miles per hour (89 km/h).

The oil embargo ended in 1974. However, the Arab nations that set the embargo realized their power. In order to profit most from their oil, they continue to work together to limit oil production. And until a sufficient replacement is found, oil will continue to hold great value and power.

CORN ETHANOL

Ethanol is a colorless, flammable liquid that is used in liquors and fuel. Ethanol fuel is made from various grains. **Starches** from corn, wheat, rice, and potato skins can be made into ethanol. In the United States, 95 percent of ethanol is made from corn.

Ethanol was first used in the United States in the 1850s as lamp fuel. During the American **Civil War**, there was a tax on ethanol. This made it more expensive than other fuels, such as kerosene. In response, ethanol use dropped.

Ethanol production did not pick up again until the tax was **repealed** in 1906. Two years later, automotive pioneer Henry

Ford introduced the Model T. This popular car ran on a blend of gasoline and ethanol. Still, ethanol was expensive. And in the 1920s, gasoline became the most widely used fuel.

Ford Motor Company built the Model T from 1908 until 1927. The popular car outsold all other cars for almost 20 years!

Today, there is a renewed interest in ethanol for several reasons. Blending it with gasoline means the United States can produce more fuel itself. That makes the country less dependent on other countries for **petroleum**. And compared with gasoline use, ethanol use reduces **greenhouse gas emissions** by 13 percent.

Throughout the United States, there are more than 100 ethanol production plants. The ethanol industry creates over 130,000 jobs.

Yet, not all vehicles can run on ethanol. Regular vehicles can use gasoline that contains up to 10 percent ethanol. Only special, flexible-fuel vehicles can burn E85. E85 is a blend of 85 percent ethanol and 15 percent gasoline. This fuel is not yet widely available at U.S. gas stations.

Even when ethanol is available, it has disadvantages. Ethanol contains less energy than gasoline. In fact, one gallon (4 L) of ethanol contains only 66 percent of the energy in one gallon of gasoline. That means flexible-fuel vehicles can travel fewer miles per gallon than similar gasoline-fueled vehicles.

ENERGY BUZZ
Since 2006, all gasoline sold in the United States must contain at least 2.78 percent ethanol.

Ethanol has other drawbacks, too. Most farm machinery runs on diesel fuel. So, the process of growing corn for ethanol burns **fossil fuels**. This contributes to **global warming**. In addition, corn requires plenty of fertilizer, which is often obtained from fossil fuels. Also, increased demand for corn to make ethanol raises global corn prices. So, consumers must pay more for products such as corn tortillas and corn-fed beef.

Even if all the corn grown in the United States were turned into ethanol, it would replace only 15 percent of the gasoline Americans use. Ethanol also costs a lot of money to produce. Only tax **subsidies** or very high gasoline prices make ethanol competitive with gasoline.

ENERGY GAIN OR LOSS?

Ethanol is at the center of a critical energy discussion. This fuel pumps out plenty of energy. Yet, it takes energy to grow corn and to produce ethanol from corn.

Many people wonder if ethanol pumps out more energy than it takes to make it. To answer this question, researchers consider many things. It takes energy to make the fertilizer that cornfields require. Farm machinery uses energy to plant and harvest corn. And, ethanol production plants require energy to operate. Finally, energy is needed to transport ethanol from plants to gas stations.

There are other factors, too. How many bushels of corn are harvested from a single acre (0.4 ha)? Some fields may yield only 125 bushels per acre. Others may yield more than 200. What source of energy is the ethanol plant using? Is it a nonrenewable source, such as coal or natural gas? Or is it a renewable source, such as manure?

Most experts agree that corn-based ethanol produces almost 25 percent more energy than is used to make it. And as new technologies improve ethanol production, that percentage is likely to increase.

GRAINS TO ETHANOL

An average bushel of corn contains 72,800 kernels. This amount can produce nearly 3 gallons (11 L) of ethanol.

Perhaps you're wondering how grains can be turned into ethanol. It takes the help of proteins called enzymes and organisms called yeasts.

Corn ethanol begins as corn kernels. Inside each kernel, **starch** molecules are bound together. To make ethanol, these molecules must be separated. This is when enzymes take over.

Enzymes break down the starch molecules into simple sugar molecules. Our bodies also use enzymes to break down starchy food, such as pasta, into sugars. Those sugars give us energy.

Next, the sugar molecules are **fermented**. That requires yeasts, which are tiny organisms related to fungi. The tiny yeast organisms munch on the sugar molecules and multiply themselves. In the process, they produce two substances. One is **carbon dioxide**. The other is ethanol.

Our bodies also have yeasts. Most of the time we don't notice them. But sometimes they get out of control. For example, one yeast found on the scalp can grow too much and cause a skin reaction called dandruff.

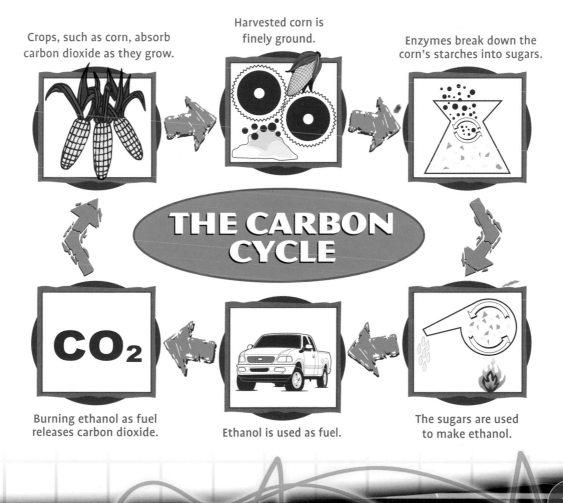

Crops, such as corn, absorb carbon dioxide as they grow.

Harvested corn is finely ground.

Enzymes break down the corn's starches into sugars.

THE CARBON CYCLE

Burning ethanol as fuel releases carbon dioxide.

Ethanol is used as fuel.

The sugars are used to make ethanol.

CELLULOSIC ETHANOL

Grains are not the only raw materials that can be used to make ethanol. Researchers are also experimenting with producing ethanol from materials that take little to no energy to grow. This would make ethanol even more energy positive.

That is the theory behind cellulosic (sehl-yuh-LOH-sihk) ethanol. Cellulosic ethanol is made from cellulose, or plant fiber, instead of grain **starch**. Advanced bioethanol technology can obtain the sugars from woody parts of plants, such as stems or leaves. Those sugars can then be turned into ethanol.

Researchers believe cellulosic ethanol has an even brighter future than grain ethanol. Cellulosic ethanol provides about 80 percent more energy than it takes to make it. And, producing it is a

Miscanthus, a native grass in Africa and southern Asia, requires much less water than many other grasses. So, it is an ideal plant for cellulosic ethanol production.

way to make fuel from inexpensive, readily available materials. In fact, grasses, wood chips, and even paper waste can all be made into cellulosic ethanol.

Greenhouse gas emissions are reduced 80 percent or more when using cellulosic ethanol instead of gasoline. And compared

Cellulose is the most abundant organic material on Earth. Many companies have recognized its value. A company called Novozymes is a leader in producing enzyme solutions that convert cellulose into simple sugars.

with corn, certain plants used to make cellulosic ethanol require much less fertilizer and **pesticides**.

Cellulosic ethanol may sound too good to be true. However, the challenge is figuring out how to produce it for less money. With current technology, a cellulosic ethanol production plant costs three times as much as a corn ethanol plant.

Yet, researchers are planning ways to reduce this cost. One way is to make plant materials **decompose** better. A possible solution

Scientists are studying the way termites digest cellulose to learn efficient methods of producing cellulosic ethanol.

is to use a type of fungus that ate away at the tents of **World War II** soldiers. That same nasty fungus may someday be the ticket to cheaper cellulosic ethanol.

Fuel from perennial grasses, such as switchgrass, could replace more than one-third of America's petroleum needs by 2030. In January 2007, President George W. Bush looked at samples of switchgrass during a visit to an alternative energy research station.

BIODIESEL

Soybean plant

Biodiesel is a fuel that can be made from plant oil, animal fat, or grease. In the United States, most biodiesel is made from soybean oil. But, the fuel can even be made with used cooking oil. In 1997, two people drove across the United States in a van that ran only on used restaurant vegetable oil.

Like ethanol, biodiesel has been around for more than 100 years. In 1893, German engineer Rudolf Diesel described his plans for a new engine that would operate using peanut oil. The engine became known as the diesel engine. However, Diesel's engine design was modified in the 1920s to run on a newer, cheaper, more plentiful fuel. That fuel was made from **petroleum**.

Modern diesel engines can run on blends of biodiesel and regular diesel fuel. Biodiesel reduces the **emissions** from those engines. In fact, biodiesel **emits** 78 percent less **carbon dioxide** than regular diesel fuel.

Biodiesel has many advantages. It is even more **efficient** to produce than cellulosic ethanol. For example, soybean biodiesel provides 93 percent more energy than the amount of energy needed to make it. And compared with **fossil fuels**, biodiesel reduces **greenhouse gas** emissions by 41 percent.

In 2005, about 75 million gallons (284 million L) of biodiesel were consumed in the United States.

Biodiesel has disadvantages, too. Consumers pay about twice as much for biodiesel, compared with regular diesel fuel. And, it can be inconvenient to use. Only a handful of drive-up pumps offer biodiesel. Sometimes, biodiesel doesn't work well in cold temperatures. In addition, biodiesel still **emits** about the same amount of smog-causing **nitrogen** oxide as regular diesel fuel.

Oil palm trees have tiny flowers that develop into clusters of fruits. To obtain the oil from the fruits, the outer part of the fruit is steamed and pressed.

Biodiesel also requires more planting. For example, one acre (0.4 ha) of soybeans can produce about 60 gallons (230 L) of biodiesel. In comparison, one acre of corn can make about 420 gallons (1,590 L) of ethanol.

Outside the United States, biodiesel production is creating more **environmental** problems than it is solving. Water surrounding biodiesel plants is often polluted, which harms or kills fish. And, farmers have cleared thousands of acres of land to plant oil palm trees. In Indonesia, rainforest loss for oil palms has contributed to the **endangerment** of more than 100 species of land animals.

CLEAN SCHOOL BUS USA

A program from the U.S. Environmental Protection Agency (EPA) aims to reduce student exposure to pollution and diesel exhaust from school buses.

BUS FACTS: In the United States, 24 million children ride school buses every day. And each year, school buses drive more than 4 billion miles (6 billion km).

PROBLEM: Most school buses use outdated diesel engines. In fact, about one-third of all buses on the roads today were built before 1990.

Using biodiesel is one way to help reduce school bus pollution.

HEALTH CONCERNS: Diesel exhaust has been linked with asthma, heart disease, and cancer. Studies show this pollution can concentrate inside school buses. This puts riders at risk.

BENEFITS: The Clean School Bus USA Program offers grants and assistance to school districts to help them clean up their buses. Some schools in the program are using new, pollution-reducing technologies for older buses. Others have purchased buses that produce less pollution. Still others have started using cleaner fuels, such as biodiesel.

HIGHLIGHTS: In 2006, the EPA awarded more than $7 million to 35 school districts nationwide for projects designed to lower diesel emissions from school buses.

GARBAGE GAS

The average American generates nearly five pounds (2 kg) of waste every day. Most of that waste ends up in landfills. Landfills, or garbage dumps, are places where garbage is buried in the ground and left to **decompose**.

But, garbage does not have to be left to rot. It can be used for energy! More and more places nationwide are producing fuel from this unwanted, yet renewable, source.

In the United States, 55 percent of garbage is placed in landfills. The other 45 percent is either recycled or burned.

Bacteria help break down most landfill garbage. In the process, a combination of **carbon dioxide** and **methane** is released. In fact, landfills are the largest source of methane **emissions** in the United States.

If left alone, methane from landfills escapes into the atmosphere. This **intensifies global warming**. But it does not have to. Some landfills are set up to capture methane for fuel production.

As with all energy sources, landfill gas has downsides. Setting up landfills to capture **methane emissions** is expensive. Transporting the captured gas also costs money. Plus, a landfill cannot generate as much energy as a coal-fired power plant. So, energy companies may not bother with an energy source that does not provide sufficient power for their customers.

Methane can be collected, treated, and sold at landfills. Or, it can be burned to generate steam and electricity.

USEFUL WASTE

Garbage is not the only waste product that can be turned into fuel. Animal waste, or manure, is also a good source of **methane**.

In the past, most livestock farmers spread manure from their animals on their fields. It worked as a fertilizer, keeping the

Waste from animals, such as cows, might one day power your home!

soil productive. Yet as farmers began raising more animals, their fields could no longer absorb all the manure. And when manure runs off of fields, it becomes a pollutant.

Today, many cattle, hog, and poultry operations produce too much manure for local farmlands. So, operators collect the extra manure in large storage tanks called lagoons. At some of these lagoons, machines called methane digesters are used to generate energy.

Methane digesters create just the right conditions for turning animal waste into energy. These machines work a lot like landfills. **Bacteria** break down the manure, and methane is released in the

process. Then, the methane is separated from the waste. It can be used to generate electricity for the farm. Or, it can be sold to electric companies.

In the United States, methane digesters keep 66,000 tons (60,000 t) of methane from escaping into the atmosphere each year. At the same time, the digesters generate enough energy to power more than 20,000 homes.

There are more than 100 methane digesters operating in the United States. And, another 80 are in the planning stages.

Some people believe methane digesters could eventually power more than 560,000 homes. And, the digesters could keep more than 1 million tons (900,000 t) of methane out of the atmosphere!

Cities such as San Francisco, California, are planning ways to turn dog waste into energy. There are about 120,000 dogs in San Francisco, and animal waste makes up almost 4 percent of residential garbage.

However, **methane** digesters are expensive to build and to operate. Therefore, power produced by digesters costs more than power from other sources. That makes many electric companies less likely to purchase methane produced from waste.

In addition, methane digesters are only valuable if there are a lot of animals to provide manure. Some people fear this encourages livestock operations to become too large. That, in turn, creates more pollution and may eliminate smaller operations. As concerns regarding pollution increase and technology is improved, renewable fuels are likely to become more widely used.

Some farmers use methane produced from digesters to provide electricity in their barns. Other farmers sell the methane. Sometimes, it generates power at ethanol plants or other renewable fuels production plants.

Renewable? Yes. New? No.

Renewable fuels are anything but new. Humans have been working for years to create energy from common, everyday materials. Low-cost oil sidetracked that quest in the early 1900s. Today, efforts to use these resources have resumed.

 1826 American inventor Samuel Morey made an engine that ran partly on ethanol.

 1900 German engineer Rudolf Diesel ran a new engine on peanut oil at the World's Fair in Paris, France.

 1908 American automaker Henry Ford unveiled the Model T car. It ran on ethanol made from corn and a fibrous plant called hemp.

1940 Henry Ford closed his Midwest ethanol plant, when interest in inexpensive oil grew.

 1973 An embargo on oil sales reduced the amount of oil available to U.S. consumers. Around the world, gasoline prices jumped. More people thought about renewable fuels.

Gasoline prices reached their peak between 1972 and 1998. They declined in the next few years.

1981

There were 163 ethanol plants in the United States. Just over a year later, only 74 were left.

1984

A boat running on pure biodiesel made its way around the world.

1996

With continued ethanol production growth, ethanol accounted for 3 percent of the total U.S. fuel consumption.

2006

GLOSSARY

bacteria - tiny, one-celled organisms that can only be seen through a microscope.

carbon dioxide - a heavy, fireproof, colorless gas that is formed when fuel containing the element carbon is burned.

civil war - a war between groups in the same country. The United States of America and the Confederate States of America fought a civil war from 1861 to 1865.

decompose - to break down into simpler parts.

efficient - the ability to produce a desired result, especially without wasting time or energy.

emit - to give off or out. An emission is something that has been emitted.

endangerment - the state of being in danger of becoming extinct.

environment - all the surroundings that affect the growth and well-being of a living thing.

ferment - to undergo a gradual chemical change in which substances, especially bacteria or yeast, change sugar into alcohol and produce carbon dioxide.

fossil fuel - a fuel that is formed in the earth from the remains of plants or animals. Coal, oil, and natural gas are fossil fuels.

global warming - an increase in the average temperature of Earth's surface.

greenhouse gas - a gas, such as carbon dioxide, that traps heat in the atmosphere.

intensify - to make something exist in a more extreme degree.

methane - a colorless, odorless, flammable gas that is formed naturally when organic matter decomposes. It is a greenhouse gas.

nitrogen - a colorless, odorless, tasteless gas that is the most plentiful element in Earth's atmosphere and is found in all living matter. Nitrogen oxide is any of several compounds of nitrogen and oxygen. It is considered a pollutant of the atmosphere.

pesticide - a chemical used to kill insects.

petroleum - a thick, dark-colored liquid that is a fossil fuel. It can be refined to make fuel and other products, such as plastics, fertilizers, and drugs.

refine - to purify. A refinery is the building and the machinery for purifying products, such as petroleum.

repeal - to formally withdraw or cancel.

starch - a white, granular, organic chemical that is produced by all green plants. It is found in the seeds of plants such as corn, wheat, and rice.

subsidy - a government's grant to a person or a company to assist in an undertaking thought helpful to the public.

World War II - from 1939 to 1945, fought in Europe, Asia, and Africa. Great Britain, France, the United States, the Soviet Union, and their allies were on one side. Germany, Italy, Japan, and their allies were on the other side.

WEB SITES

To learn more about renewable fuels, visit ABDO Publishing Company on the World Wide Web at **www.abdopublishing.com**. Web sites about renewable fuels are featured on our Book Links page. These links are routinely monitored and updated to provide the most current information available.

INDEX